Chapter 1: Introduction to Economic Theory

What is Economics?

The Economic situation of the country is always heard in the news but a few people really know what Economics is. Many are becoming interested in Economics but not in the study of it. The student now is challenged to familiarize himself with what Economics is about. He will now learn how to analyze Economic theory and to explain the different issues, situations and phenomena happening in the country's economy. With the increase interest and emphasis in Economics, it is truly commendable for a person to be equipped with the knowledge on how the Economy runs.

Economics is a broad ranging discipline that uses a variety of techniques and approaches to address important social questions (Leaño, Jr. & Corpuz, 2005). Economics comes from the Greek word *"oikanomia"* meaning "Household Management." Economics, being a broad discipline, has many definitions as follows:

a. It is the proper allocation and efficient use of available resources for the maximum satisfaction of human wants (Fajardo, 1999).
b. It is the study of how man could best allocate and utilize scarce resources of society to satisfy man's unlimited wants (Castillo, 1989).
c. According to the Webster Dictionary, Economics is a branch of knowledge that deals with the production, distribution and consumption of goods and services.

Based on these definitions, we could safely say that Economics is a social science concerned with the allocation and efficient utilization of available scarce resources for the satisfaction of man's unlimited needs and wants. This is a general definition of Economics that economists accept.

The definition that we will be using for this term is this: **Economics is a social science that studies the activities of man and the satisfaction of man's unlimited material needs and wants through the allocation of scarce resources.**

Man, by nature, is difficult to satisfy and has changing material needs and wants. Man's needs become more sophisticated, complex, and increase in quality and quantity.

Why study Economics?

Many individuals have no clear understanding of what Economics truly is. People just do not mind to know what it is, how it works and how it affects their lives. Here's the thing, No individual can isolate himself from economics. This is due to the fact that an individual's physical existence greatly depends upon economics. None of us can live without production and consumption. Almost all of man's activities involve economics like the buying and selling of goods, earning money for a living, and the like. These are examples of *Economic Activities.*

It is clear that knowledge of economics is quite favorable for an individual to have. It can be a guide for living, how one can be thrifty not just in using money but with all materials available in this world, how one can run a business properly for it to become profitable and successful, how to deal with the scarcity of resources, and the like. Economics can make living simple and, likely better for everyone.

In the study of Economics, we must remember that it is a science. The principles of which are arrived at only after the tedious process of observations, experimentations, and empirical testing. And it is not just a science but a social science which studies man's life and how an individual lives with other persons. It studies man's behavior as a producer and consumer.

Let's be clear that this course will not make you an economist but you will surely learn how to pose and deal with questions in ways that will help produce and arrive at rational, feasible, and economically acceptable answers. In this course, you, the student is expected to be able to: (1) Identify regular and persistent human economic behavior, (2) Predict human economic behavior, and (3) Formulate patterns of economic behavior

This is not the way in solving economic problems though this could be a start. We must keep in mind that in the posing of economic problems the solutions proposed must also be economic in nature. But economic problems are not purely economic in nature. There are also non-economic factors that form economic problems like education, poverty, politics, culture and the like.

 **Activity 1: Man's material needs and wants**

Identify and classify your material needs and wants.

NEEDS	WANTS
= are based on physiological, personal or socio-economic requirements necessary for you to function and live	= these are goods that are beyond man' needs

NEEDS		WANTS	
1.	6.	1.	6.
2.	7.	2.	7.
3.	8.	3.	8.
4.	9.	4.	9.
5.	10.	5.	10.

Activity 2: Man's focus on his wants rather than his needs

Based on your answers on Activity 1, what are your wants that you are willing to let go for you to focus on your needs. List three (3) below and cite your reasons for your action.

1.	
2.	
3.	

 **Activity 3: Man's CHANGING material needs and wants**

There are two columns in the table below. On the left column, write the goods that are becoming or have become obsolete because of an innovative product while on the column on the right, write down the innovative or upgraded products that make the products on the left obsolete.

	Obsolete Product	Innovative Product
1.		
2.		
3.		
4.		
5.		
6.		
7.		
8.		
9.		
10.		

Economic Resources

Man cannot produce goods and services without utilizing the different resources in our world. These economic resources are the inputs in the production of goods and services. They are customarily called as the *Factors of Production*.

There are four (4) generally accepted Economic Resources:

1. **Land** - This covers all the natural resources, not man-made, found on or under land. (e.g.) water, plants, animals, minerals and the like.
2. **Labor** - This covers all the human effort/man-power expended in the making of goods and services.
3. **Capital** - This covers all the man-made materials used in the processing of raw materials to create goods and services. (e.g.) money, machines, buildings and the like.
4. **Entrepreneur** - The one who puts together or organizes the other factors of production. He is the person who has used his Land, Labor and Capital to create a good or a service.

   * **Variables** - these are factors that are subject to change or are always changing

What is an Economic System?

The term Economic System simply means the organization of economic society with reference to the production, exchange, distribution and consumption of wealth (Leaño Jr. & Corpuz, 2005). It's like a framework in which a society decides on or resolves its *economic problems*. These problems are:

1. **What to Produce?**

   The system shall determine the desires of the people in a society. The goods and services produced are based on the needs and wants of the end-users or the consumers. An entrepreneur should think of products that can:
   a. compete,
   b. satisfy a need or a want, and;
   c. be produced for raw materials found nearby.

In simple terms, the answer to this question is to produce one satisfying product. This is also the main challenge to entrepreneurs more than to create competitive and cheap products.

2. **How to Produce?**

This is the knowledge on the selecting of the appropriate combination of economic resources in producing the right quantity of output. This also involves the use of technology. In selecting the technique to be used in production, an entrepreneur has to choose between using a labor intensive or a capital intensive form. *Labor intensive* means putting in more manpower while *Capital intensive* means putting in more machines or monetary investment in the production process.

3. **How much to Produce?**

The system must know the quantity of the chosen goods to be produced. It mainly depends on the desire of the people in a society, on how much the people want the product. It concerns more on the demand of the product. Taste and Preference play a big role here and a careful analysis of the "previous month's sales report" will be used to determine if one needs to produce more, produce less, or cut off the production and find a new product to produce.

4. **For whom to Produce?**

The system now determines the target market of the product. In here, the taste and preference of the consumers are keys to determine who the end users of the product are. In here, there will be times where the entrepreneur will adjust the specifications of the products to address a majority but particular consumer preference.

These four questions can be changed and adapted depending on the situation. They greatly depend on the economic system that a particular society is currently adopting or is used to.

Types of Economic Systems

1. **Traditional** - in this system people produce goods and services for their own consumption and the decisions are based on the customs and traditions of the people. There's the danger here of the continuous use of obsolete production techniques.
2. **Command** - in this system a leader, or a body of leaders takes hold of the economy of a society. The leader or the lead body dictates the policies used and also answer all the economic questions. The consumers cannot choose the goods and services that they want.
3. **Market System** - This is also called *Free Enterprise System*. Decisions regarding investments, production, and distribution are based on the supply and demand of products desired by the people. This also includes the prices of goods and services.
4. **Mixed Economy** - This is a mixture of the all the different types of economic System. This is the system that is commonly used by most of the countries including the Philippines.

What is Economic Activity?

These are the actions that involve the production, distribution and consumption of goods and services in all the levels within a society. Man's best economic activity is his continuous effort to satisfy his needs and wants with the use of goods and services.

The key factors here are that man's needs and wants are unlimited and the resources are limited. In the definition of Economics, it's indicated there that man allocates *scarce resources*. Scarcity is the main economic problem and is also the main reason for the study of economics. Scarcity does not connote shortage in supply. It connotes that resources are *limited*. It states that resources deplete and sooner or later be exhausted and not be created again. And Economic Activity is the solution not for scarcity but for the problem of distribution and allocation of these limited resources.

Economic Activity has Three (3) elements:

1. Human Needs and Wants
2. Use of Resources
3. Techniques of Production
   - Capital Intensive
   - Labor Intensive

Aside from addressing the problem of scarcity of resources, and the proper allocation and distribution of which, Economic Activity also solves the following problems:

1. Unemployment
2. Instability
3. Societal Growth and Development
4. Inequality
5. The type of Economic System to be used

Maslow's Hierarchy of Human Needs

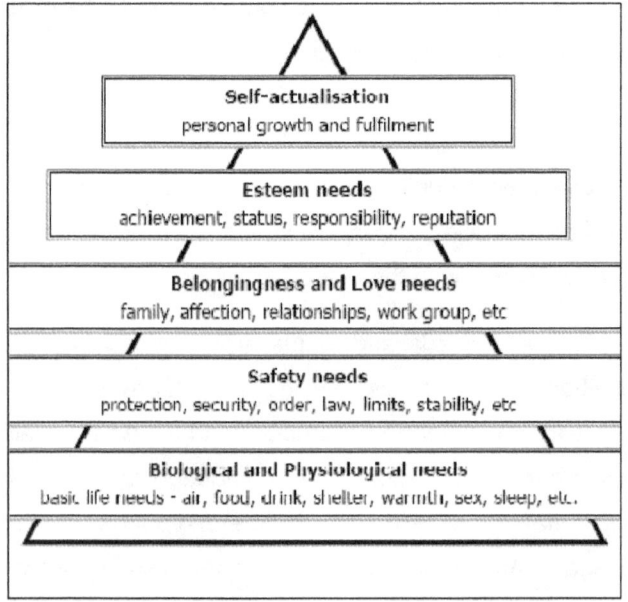

Abraham Maslow was an American Psychologist who theorized in his paper on Human Motivation that humans have different stages of curiosity through man's development and growth as he ages.

Economic Analysis

This is the process of directing economic relationships by examining economic behavior and events, and determining the causal relationships among the data and activities observed (Pagoso, et al, 2006). We must learn to analyze relationships among economic variables, quantitatively describe economic behavior, formulate hypotheses, empirically test our findings and draw conclusions from the data observed and received.

Purposes of Economic Analysis

1. To aid in understanding economic operations
2. Permits the prediction of the results of the changes in economic variables
3. Serves as basis for Basic Economic Policy Formation

Economic Tools

1. **Logic** - This involves the use of reason. There are two types of reasoning used in Economic Analysis:
    a. Inductive Reasoning
       - This is the drawing of conclusions from particulars to the general idea.
    b. Deductive Reasoning
       - This is the drawing of conclusions from the general idea down to the particular ideas of which.
2. **Statistics** - This is the quantitative description of economic behavior. This is the basis for hypothesis testing.
3. **Mathematics** - This is the quantifying process of the hypothesis for it to be empirically verified.

The Science of Economics

Economics as a science involves verifying data observed through the use of economic analysis and the economic tools used by it. It is a science that provides a systematic body of knowledge offering solutions and insights to basic problem of unlimited wants versus scarce resources. There are four (4) distinct steps in the method used in economic analysis (also known as the Scientific Method in Economics) and these are:

1. **Observation**
   - This is the determination of problems observed in the society and the prioritization of which should be given immediate solution or solutions. This is due to the drive of some economists to pursue and define the "Main Problem" in the economy of a particular country.
2. **Definitions and Assumptions**
   - This is the definition of terms. Assumptions, on the other hand, are the variables or components that need to be put into consideration.
3. **Inductive or Deductive Reasoning to arrive at conclusions**
   - This involves mathematical and logical reasoning. There are two ways in presenting the proponent's reasons Inductive, and Deductive Reasoning. There are errors reasoning that must be avoided to arrive at accurate and appropriate conclusions. These are called *fallacies in reasoning*. Here are some examples of fallacies:
     a. **Fallacy of Mere Antecedent**
        - An event occurred immediately before another event and the first event is assumed as the cause of the second event even if there are no clear proofs of it or even of the relationship (if there is) of the two events.
     b. **Fallacy of Begging the Question**
        - This is committed when one assumes something (an idea) as proven even if it's yet to be proven so.

c. **Fallacy of Sweeping Generalization**
   - This is committed when one concludes that what is 'TRUE' for a one or a few individuals in a group is also true for all the members of the group.
d. **Fallacy of Emotionalism**
   - This is committed when the reasoning greatly appeals to and carries much emotion, and that it does not present facts and evidences of general applications. This cannot pass the test of logic that is why it must be avoided.
e. **Fallacy of Composition**
   - This is committed when the proponent argues that is true for some of the parts of a particular area is also true for the entirety or the whole of which.

4. **Empirical and Statistical Testing**

   This uses the tools of economics: (1) Logic, (2) Mathematics, and (3) Statistics. Logic is used in deriving conclusions from the data gathered while Mathematics and Statistics facilitate derivation of conclusions through the use of numbers and quantitative analysis. Statistics make the qualified data into quantifiable data which what is acceptable in the derivation or drawing of conclusions and drafting of recommendations.

The Circular Flow of Economic Activity

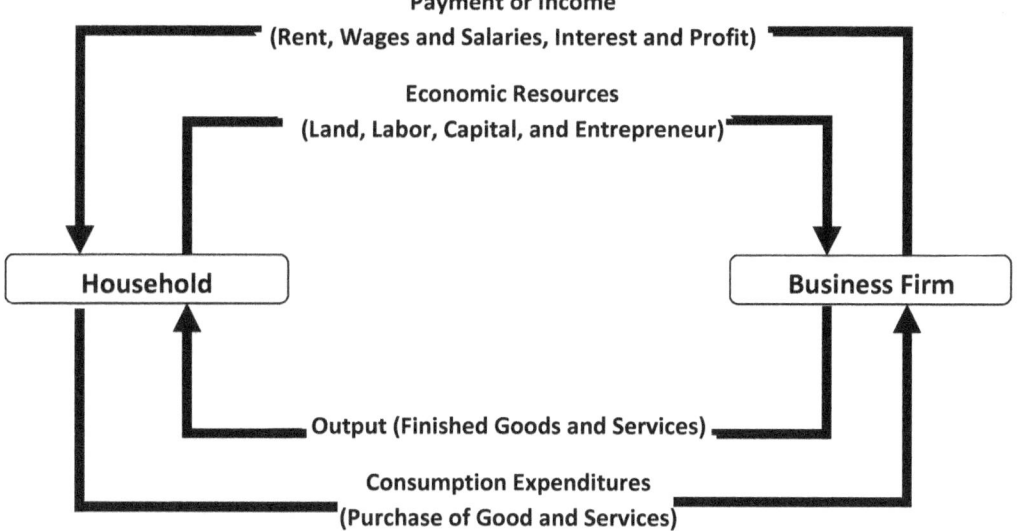

There are two factors or sectors that we can clearly see in the diagram: the Household and the Business Firm. The Circular Flow shows us the what, when, where and how the two factors interact and come to the activity of *Production*. In the diagram, it is clear that the Business Firm is the producer and that the Household is the end-user of the goods and services produced by the Business Firm. (Upper half of the diagram) The Household is the source of the resources used by the Business Firm to produce final goods and in return the Household receives Payment or Income for the resources they have given for production. On the lower half of the diagram, we see there the buyer-seller relationship of the Household and the Business Firm. The Household needs to make a purchase to be able to get the benefits and be satisfied by the final good/services produced by the Business Firm.

The Production and Consumption Flow, and the Financial Flow

The Production and Consumption Flow   - Starts at the Household and also ends at the Household

The Financial Flow   - Starts at the Business Firm and ends also at the Business Firm

Activity 1: Scarcity: The basic and central problem of economics

Briefly explain how you can apply economics in your daily life in the following situations:

a. Time Management

_____
_____
_____
_____

b. Daily/Weekly/Monthly Allowance

_____
_____
_____
_____

c. Food/Drink

___

Activity 2: Sample Economic Analysis

Based on your personal observation, make a short discussion of the current status of the Philippine Economy. Use the following as sample topics as a jumpstart for your discussion: Poverty, Social Unrest, Foreign Exchange, Government Economic Policies and Laws.

Activity 3: Matching Type.

Find Context Clues to correctly match items from column B to column A. Write only the letter of your answers on the space provided.

_____ 1. Traditional Market

_____ 2. Financial Flow

_____ 3. Fallacy of Mere Antecedent

_____ 4. Economic Analysis

_____ 5. Inductive Reasoning

_____ 6. Mixed Economy

_____ 7. Variables

_____ 8. Land

_____ 9. Capital

_____ 10. Economic System

_____ 11. Emotionalism

_____ 12. Logic

_____ 13. Physiological Needs

_____ 14. Assumptions

_____ 15. Mathematics

a. the first event is assumed as the cause of the second event.

b. starts from the particular ideas ending with the general idea

c. the widely used type of economic system

d. a framework wherein society decides on their economic problems

e. all the man-made materials used in production

f. factors that are always changing

g. examining Economic Behavior

h. all the natural materials used in production

i. starts and end w/ the Business Firm

j. customary form of system

k. Food, shelter, clothing, sex, warmth

l. Variables to be considered in analysis

m. The quantification of the hypothesis for empirical verification

n. Reasoning that greatly appeal to the emotions of people.

o. This involves the use of reason.

Take Home Activity: Economic System

Among the types of Economic Systems identified. Which do you think is best for our economy? Explain your answer in not less than ten (10) sentences.

Chapter 2: MICROECONOMICS: The Price Theory

Two Branches of Economics

Macroeconomics   - This branch of economics studies the economy as a whole.

- This is also known as *National Income Analysis*.

Microeconomics   - This branch of economics deals with the parts of an economy, i.e. the household.

- This is also known as the *Price Theory*.

Microeconomics

This is the branch of economics with the individual decisions of units of the economy—firms, households, and how their choices determine relative prices of goods and factors of production (Marcelino, et al. 2010). It is the economic analysis of the market behavior individual consumers and firms in an attempt to understand the decision-making processes of households and firms.

Characteristics of Microeconomics: (Pagoso, et al, 2006)

1. Microeconomics looks at the decisions of individual units.
2. Microeconomics looks at how prices are determined.
3. Microeconomics is concerned with social welfare.
4. Microeconomics has a limited focus.
5. Microeconomics help develop the skills of logical reasoning, the construction and use of economic models, decision making for a variety of situations, and the proper allocation of personal resources.

Core Ideas of Microeconomics

1. **Supply**   - The quantity of available products (goods and services) for a certain price.
2. **Demand**   - The quantity of a product (a good or a service) that consumers desire.

3. **Market Equilibrium** - this refers to a condition where a market price is established through competition such that the amount of goods or services sought by buyers is equal to the amount of goods or services produced by sellers.

Classification of Human Needs

1. **Basic Needs**   - food, shelter, and clothing
2. **Essential Needs** - goods that man needs to live comfortably, i.e. appliances
3. **Public Needs**   - public transportation, schools, hospitals
4. **Luxury Needs**   - goods that are beyond being basic and essential, i.e. cellular phones, laptops, and the like

Mixed Economy

The market is the main focus of the study of Microeconomics. In the Market Economy, consumers are free to choose what goods and services they will purchase within the limits of their income. This means individuals have the right to property and with this, they gain the ability to buy, to sell and establish their own businesses. In the system of Mixed Economy, there is this mixture of the three other economic system types. In here, the Microeconomic function of being concerned with the flow of goods and services from business firms to consumers, the composition of the flow, and the process for establishing the relative prices of the component parts of the flow is easily seen because of it clearly follows the Circular Flow.

 Take Home Activity: Research on the Classification of Needs

Why is water **not** classified into any of the types of needs?

Activity 1: Microeconomics
Write only the letter of the best answer.

_____ 1. This refers to the quantity of available products for a certain price.
   a. Demand
   b. Supply
   c. Equilibrium
   d. None of these

_____ 2. These are the needs that are beyond being basic and essential to man.
   a. Essential
   b. Basic
   c. Luxury
   d. Wants

_____ 3. What is the other term for National Income Analysis?
   a. Economics
   b. Microeconomics
   c. Gross Domestic Product
   d. Macroeconomics

_____ 4. Which is not true about Microeconomics?
   a. It looks at the behavior of firms and of the household
   b. It studies the economy as a whole
   c. It is concerned with social welfare
   d. It looks at how prices are determined

_____ 5. What is the other term for Microeconomics?
   a. Price Theory
   b. Law of Price
   c. Circular Flow
   d. Outflow Theory

_____ 6. This happens when Supply and Demand are equal.
   a. Market Stability
   b. Market Economy
   c. Market Equilibrium
   d. Market System

_____ 7. These are the needs that are usually provided by the state and government.
   a. Luxury Needs
   b. Public Needs
   c. Basic Needs
   d. Personal Needs

_____ 8. This type of economic system is a mixture of the 3 basic economic systems.
   a. Mixed Economy
   b. Mixed Production
   c. Mixed Market
   d. Mixed Equilibrium

_____ 9. This branch of Economics studies the economy as a whole.
   a. Microeconomics
   b. Macroeconomics
   c. Maicroeconomics
   d. Maecroeconomics

_____ 10. This is the quantity of a product that a consumer desires.
   a. Supply
   b. Equilibrium
   b. Market price
   d. Demand

Chapter 3: DEMAND AND SUPPLY

The Law of Demand

This Law states that as Demand goes up Prices go down. There is an inversely proportional relationship between Price and Demand. This means as prices of the good or service decreases, people will buy more of that said good or service.

The Demand Curve

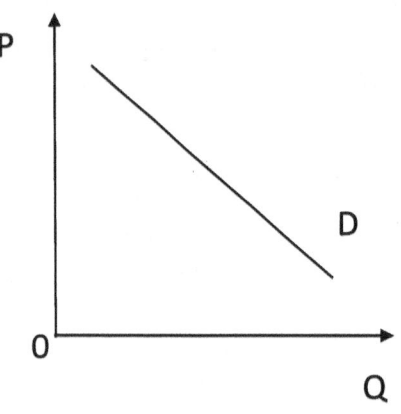

The demand curve is downward sloping, indicating the negative relationship between the price of a product and the quantity demanded.

Changes in the Demand Curve

1. **Change in Price**

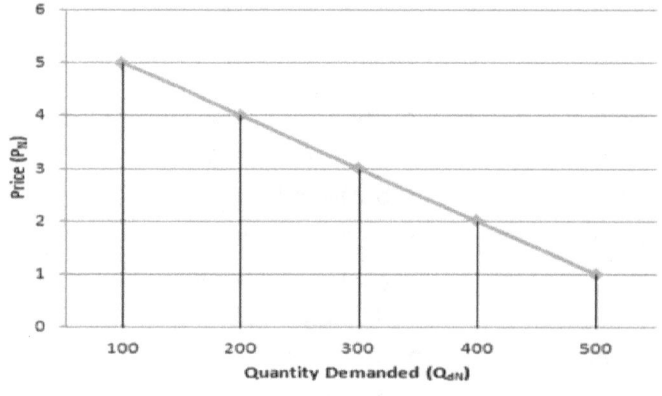

This results in movement along the demand curve.

2. Change in a Non-Price Variable

a. For a Normal Good

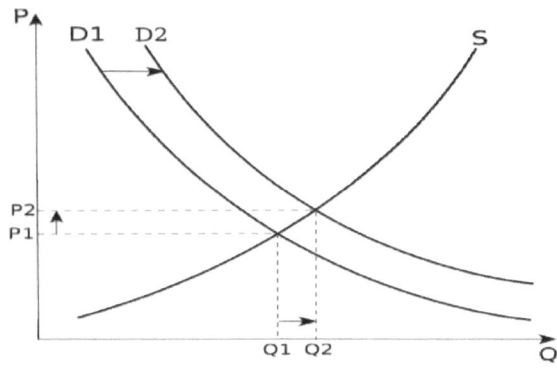

There is an outward shift in the demand curve due to the increase of income of the consumers. The increase of income meaning more money to buy more of their needs and wants.

b. For an Inferior Good

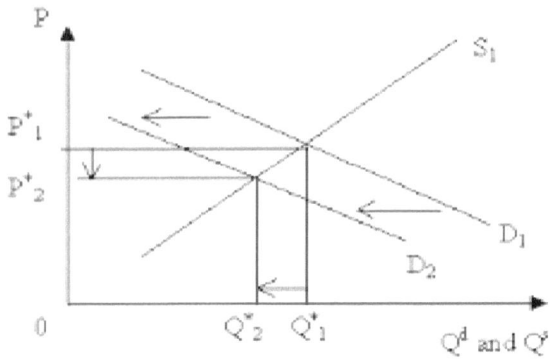

There is an inward shift in the demand curve even if there is an increase of income because consumers will choose the superior good over the inferior good.

Hypothetical Goods that do not follow the Law of Demand

1. Giffen Goods

These are inferior goods that are mere substitutes for more expensive goods which, people buy more when they cannot afford the superior goods.

2. Veblen Goods

These are goods that people buy because they are expensive and also for show of wealth.

The Law of Supply

This Law states that as Price increases, Supply also increases. This connotes a positive relationship between Price and Supply. As the Price of a good goes up, the available supply of a good increases because higher prices mean lower demand of the product and lower demand means less people who are buying the good.

The Supply Curve

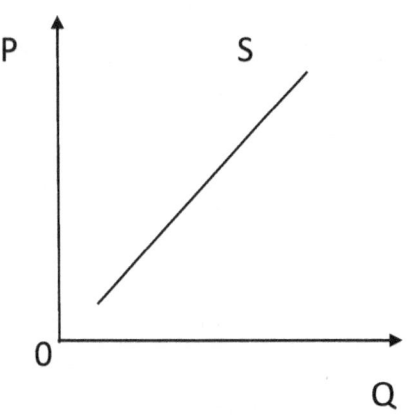

The Supply Curve is an upward sloping curve, indicating the positive relationship between the price of a product and the quantity supplied.

Changes in the Supply Curve

1. Change in Price

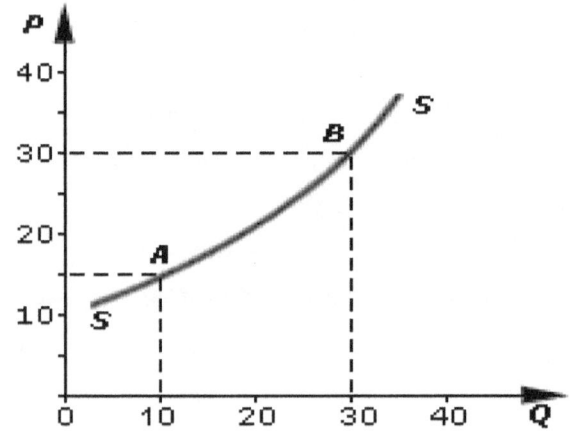

This results in movement along the Supply Curve

2. **Change in the Cost of Production**

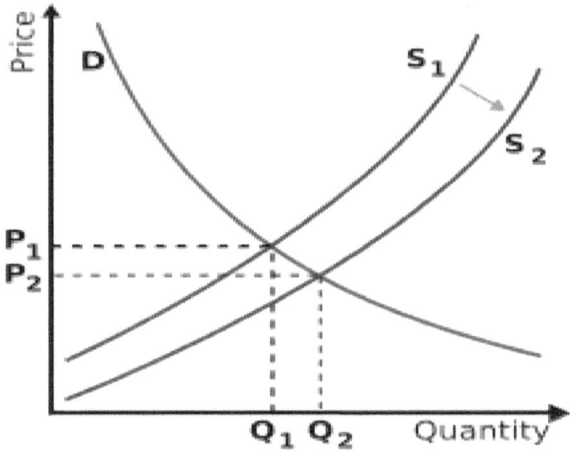

a. The supply curve will shift outward if *costs decrease*. It means more products will be produced with almost the same cost of production.

b. The supply curve will shift inward if *costs increase* which means less products will be produced due to the increase of production costs.

3. **Change in the Expected Demand**

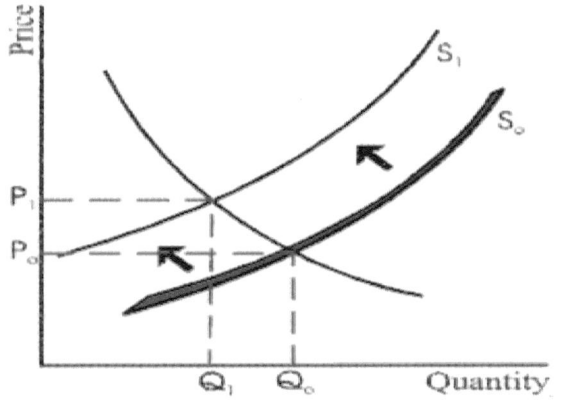

a. The supply curve will shift outward if consumer enthusiasm is expected to increase.

b. The supply curve will shift inward if there is an expectation for consumer preferences to change in favor of an alternative good or service.

Equilibrium

This happens when the supply and demand curves intersect, the market is in equilibrium. This is where the quantity demanded and the quantity supplied are equal.

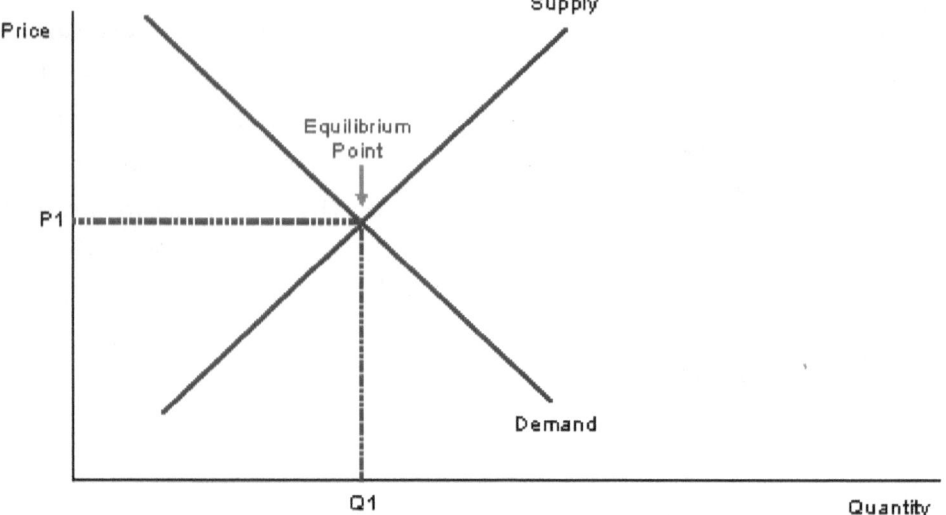

In reaching *Economic Equilibrium*, it assumes that all other external forces are constant, and economic variables are constant. Economic Equilibrium is the goal of Economic Activity—to reach a point where there is a steady supply of goods satisfying the demand of the consumers. It's quite impossible to achieve this because there shall be points where surpluses or shortages shall be incurred. Another is it is quite hard to maintain equilibrium even for a short period of time. Most producers look at equilibrium as a mere breakeven for them which make them eager to incur surpluses to increase their income.

It is the job of the government to reach equilibrium but it is a collective effort for the government is considered as an outside force in the circular flow of resources in economics. But there are ways the government enforces its will to regulate the economy and economic activity. We call these *Government Intervention* wherein the government creates policies which they enforce to protect public interest and to maintain (if there is) market and economic stability.

Government Intervention

This is the action done by the government to combat if not prevent market inequities and promote fairness. This is to protect the local market. When we speak of local market, it consists of the consumers (buyers), the sellers, and the producers. So if the  government protects the local market, the government is pertaining to the protection of the consumers from defective, ineffective, unsatisfying, overpriced etc. products, the government is protecting the producers from not gaining the appropriate profit for their investment, and the government is protecting the sellers from not gaining profit for their exerted effort (monetary and labor) to buy and sell products. It short terms, the government protects the interest of the market's stakeholders.

There are three common interventions done by the government:
1. Taxation
2. Subsidies
3. Regulation

Taxation

 This is a system of raising money to finance the state and government. It is the supreme power of a sovereign state to impose burdens or charges upon persons, property, or property rights for public purposes. *Taxes* are the compulsory contributions to support the state.

Subsidies

 A Subsidy is benefit given by the government to groups or individuals usually in the form of a cash payment or tax reduction. The subsidy is usually given to remove some type of burden and is often considered to be in the interest of the public (http://www.investopedia.com).

It is a remedy done by the government to protect the market and its stakeholders from either high market prices or high local taxes which they would cover or lessen for them by giving a form of discount in either taxes or processing fees.

An example of this would be the subsidy given by the government to the National Food Authority for them to sell NFA rice at the lowest possible selling price.

Regulation

Regulations are done by the government to promote economic fairness. Sometimes these are done to promote national unity and state advancement. This is the use of legislative measures and government regulations to affect economic outcomes. This can extend from forms of government that control and regulate all aspects of economics to measures which are enacted to address particular issues such as deregulation of industries or measures intended to address various economic factors (http://www.businessdictionary.com/). An example of regulation done by the government is Price Control.

1. Price Control
    a. Price Ceiling
        - The establishment of a maximum price for a good/service or certain goods or services to protect consumers.
        - The government wants to ensure the good is affordable for as many consumers as possible.
    b. Price Floor
        - The establishment of a minimum price for a good/service or some goods or services to protect producers of said goods and services.
        - A government wants to ensure the good is profitable for as many producers as possible.

In effecting Price Control regulations, there are these byproducts or side effects of it in the economy. They can be deemed positive, negative or both depending on the point of view of the economic stakeholder. In Price Ceiling, there is the danger of shortages of goods. The producers of the controlled good are not reaching profitable or not even break even status for their good that is why they lessen their production for them to still gain some profit. In Price Floor, on the other hand, there is surplus. Surpluses are excess goods that are either left on the shelves, or in warehouses of both the sellers and producers. There are three types of surplus. First is Supply surplus. *Supply surpluses* are the excess good which are generally added to the producer's inventory. If there is an increase in supply surplus that would mean that sooner or later product prices would decrease for the excess to be sold. Worse is when there is truly a large amount of supply surplus that would mean that supply or production must halt for there is much of that product in the market and that is not a profitable situation. That could lead to factory foreclosure. Second is Consumer surplus. *Consumer surplus* is the gain obtained by consumers because they can obtain a product for a lower price than they would be willing to pay. This could be in the form of a bargain. Because of the decrease in the price of a product, consumers will now be able to buy more of that good. Lastly, we have Producer surplus. *Producer surplus* is the benefit producers get by selling at a price higher than the lowest price they would sell for. This would mean they'll be gaining more profit.

Activity 1: Demand and Supply

Graph the following points and identify whether the curve made is a supply or demand curve.

1. P1 10   Q1 30
   P2 20   Q2 20

2. P1 50   Q1 60
   P2 20   Q2 90

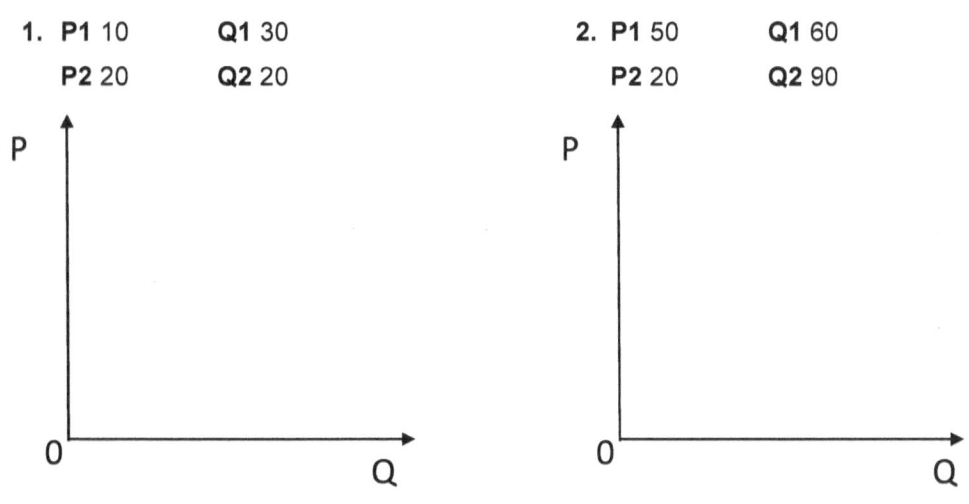

3. **P1** 75   **Q1** 100
   P2 60   **Q2** 85

4. **P1** 100   **Q1** 550
   P2 200   **Q2** 375

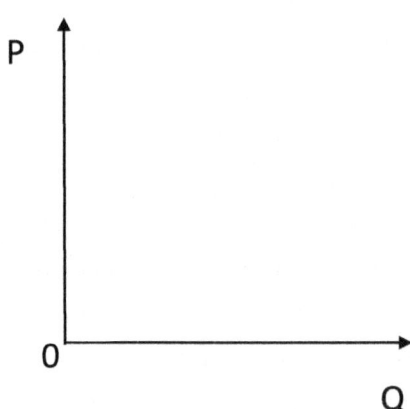

5. **P1** 5   **Q1** 15
   P2 25   **Q2** 8

6. **P1** 7.50   **Q1** 75
   P2 7.00   **Q2** 90

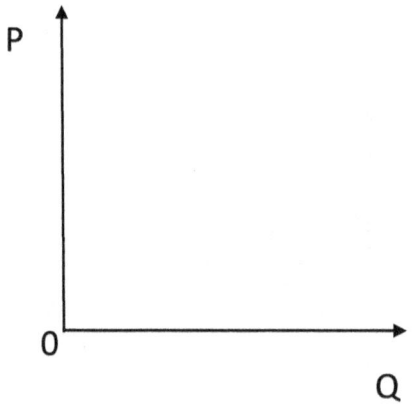
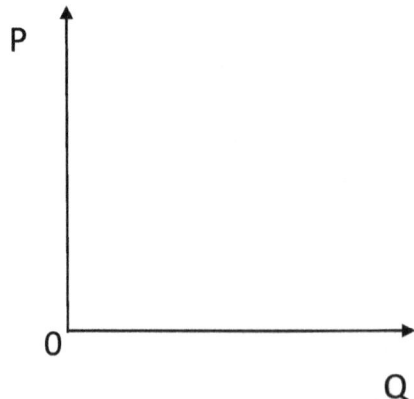

Activity 2: Demand Schedule

Plot the following hypothetical demand schedule for pork in the market:

Price of Pork (per kilo)	Quantity Demanded (in kilos)
P 175	60
160	75
150	85
125	100
105	130

P

0   Q

Activity 3: Supply Schedule

Plot the following hypothetical supply schedule of Bangus in the market:

Price of Tuna (per kilo)	Quantity Supplied (in kilos)
P 140	600
110	455
95	390
75	300
70	275

P

0   Q

Take Home Activity: Case on Regulation

Republic Act No. 8479: The Oil Deregulation Law

After the Deregulation, the oil industry became more competitive and it being more competitive, oil companies were encouraged to be more effective and efficient in terms of their advertising and product quality.

Features of the Law:
- The government cannot interfere with the pricing, export and importation of oil products, the establishment of retail outlets, storage depots, ocean-receiving facilities and refineries.
- Large business establishments and government corporations can also import their fuel requirements without securing any permit from the government; they simply have to inform the DOE of their move.

Why is there the need for Deregulation?
- To save money.
    - the government will no longer subsidize the market when prices go up.
    - tax payers' money will be used for more resolute projects and programs because it will no longer be use as a subsidy.
    - the government would be able to use public funds for vital services and infrastructure such as schools, hospitals, roads, bridges, and the like.

Guide Questions:
1. What's your first impression on the presented details of the oil deregulation law?
2. Basing on your personal observation and knowledge, is the competitive market formed by the enactment of this law healthy for the Philippine economy? Cite an example proving your answer.
3. Would you like to change some parts of the law, or would you like to repeal the law, or would you like to leave the law as it is? Explain your answer.

Case Study Format

Title: _____

I. **Point of View:**

This is the standpoint of the proponent of the case. The standpoint will determine what kind of action the proponent will undertake in doing the following:
1. Identifying the problem in the case.
2. Presenting the problem
3. Identifying the key facts of the case that confirms the problem as one problem if not the main problem of the case.
4. Proposing the courses of action
5. In choosing and recommending the proponent's best course of action
6. In preparing an action plan for the implementation of the chosen course of action.

II. **Statement of the Problem**

This is the main problem of the case in the point of view of the proponent. This should be presented in a complete sentence and should not be elaborated in this part of the case study.

III. **Facts of the Case**

This is where the proponent points out the statements in the case which proves and supports his stated problem as the key problem of the case. These facts will also be used in developing the courses of action and in choosing the best course of action among which the proponent will then create a plan in the implementation of the chosen as best course of action.

IV. **Alternative Courses of Action**

The proponent offers three different courses of action. He will then think of the advantages and disadvantages of the course of action. He can include the opportunities and threats to be faced in the future if that course of action is done.

The proponent will have to identify at least three advantages and also three disadvantages for every course of action presented.

A. 1ST OPTION

ADVANTAGES	DISADVANTAGES
•	•
•	•
•	•

B. 2ND OPTION

ADVANTAGES	DISADVANTAGES
•	•
•	•
•	•

C. 3RD OPTION

ADVANTAGES	DISADVANTAGES
•	•
•	•
•	•

V. Recommendation

The proponent chooses his choice as the best plan of action among the alternative courses of action he presented in the Alternative Courses of Action section. The recommendation should be in paragraph form. In it, the proponent identifies his chosen best course of action and also the reasons why he chose it. He can cite its advantages over the other courses of action.

VI. Plan of Action (Action Plan)

An action plan is a document that lists what steps must be taken in order to achieve a specific goal. The purpose of an action plan is to clarify what resources are required to reach the goal, formulate a timeline for when specific tasks need to be completed and determine what resources are required.

Work Plan Template

Purpose: To create a "script" for your improvement effort and support implementation.

Directions: 1. Using this form as a template, develop a work plan for each goal identified through the needs assessment process. Modify the form as needed to fit your unique context.
2. Distribute copies of each work plan to the members of the collaboration.
3. Keep copies handy to bring to meetings to review and update regularly. You may decide to develop new work plans for new phases of your reform effort.

Goal:

Results/Accomplishments:

Action Steps What Will Be Done?	Responsibilities Who Will Do It?	Timeline By When? (Day/Month)	Resources A. Resources Available B. Resources Needed (financial, human, political & other)	Potential Barriers A. What individuals or organizations might resist? B. How?	Communications Plan Who is involved? What methods? How often?
Step 1:			A. B.	A. B.	
Step 2:			A. B.	A. B.	
Step 3:			A. B.	A. B.	
Step 4:			A. B.	A. B.	
Step 5:			A. B.	A. B.	

Evidence Of Success *(How will you know that you are making progress? What are your benchmarks?)*

Evaluation Process *(How will you determine that your goal has been reached? What are your measures?)*

Elasticity of Demand and Supply

Elasticity is defined as the responsiveness of demand/supply to a change in its determinant. It is the measure used to respond to changes in the determinants of either supply/demand. We shall only be dealing with Price Elasticity in both Demand and Supply

Price Elasticity

This is degree of responsiveness of quantity demanded to a change in price. This is measured by dividing the percentage change in quantity demanded by the percentage change in price. Buyers tend to purchase more as prices decrease and purchase less as prices increase. Let us consider another example (Leaño, Jr & Corpuz, 2005):

Given:

Demand Schedule of Product X

Price	Quantity Demanded (Qd)
4	100
5	80

Q1 = 100   **P1 = 4**
Q2 = 60   **P2 = 5**

Formulas:

$$Ep = \frac{\Delta Qd}{Qd_1} \div \frac{\Delta P}{P_1} \qquad \Delta Qd = Qd_2 - Qd_1$$
$$\Delta P = P_2 - P_1$$

Solution:

$\Delta Q = 60 - 100$
$\quad = -40$
$\Delta P = 5 - 4$
$\quad = 1$

$Ep = \frac{-40}{100} \div \frac{1}{4}$
$\quad = -0.4 \div 0.25$
$Ep = \underline{-1.6}$

Note:
The price elasticity of demand has a negative sign due to the inverse relationship of price and quantity demanded. DISREGARD THE SIGN.

Elasticity Interpretation

There are five (5) reaction patterns in Price Elasticity:

1. **Elastic**

    In here, a small change in price (P) results in a large change in quantity demanded (Qd) or quantity supplied (Qs). This simply means that a one percent change in price will have more than one percent change in quantity demanded or supplied. The numerical coefficient is more than one, ≥ 1.

    Graphical representation:

    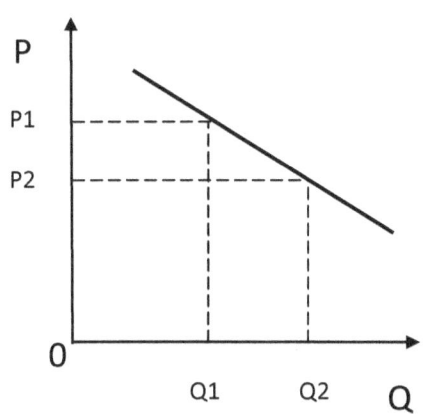

Example:

Price	Quantity Demanded (Qd)
P 18.50	100
P 25.00	25

Ep = (25 − 100) / 100   **Ep = -2.13**   *Disregard the sign*
       (25 − 18.50) / 18.50

Ep = -75 / 100   **2.13 > 1 = ELASTIC**
       6.50 / 18.50

Ep = -0.75
       0.35

2. Inelastic

In contrast to the Elastic variant, a large change in price (P) results to a lesser change in quantity demanded or supplied. This means a one percent change in price would result to a less than one percent change in quantity demanded or supplied. The numerical coefficient is less than one, ≤ 1.

Graphical representation:

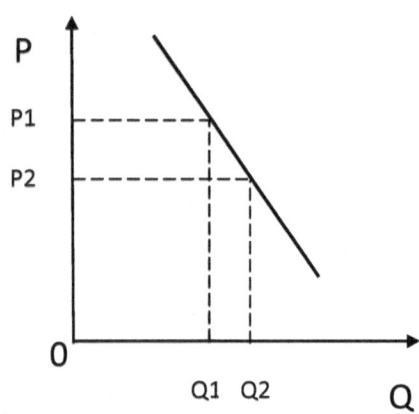

Example:

Price	Quantity Demanded (Qd)
P 100	80
P 150	90

Ep = (90 – 80) / 80   **Ep = 0.25**
 (150 – 100) / 100

Ep = 10 / 80   **0.25 < 1 = INELASTIC**
 50 / 100

Ep = 0.125
 0.5

3. **Unitary**

Demand is unitary when a percentage change in price leads to a proportionately equal percentage change in quantity demanded or supplied. The revenue remains as is. The numerical coefficient is one, = 1.

Graphical representation:

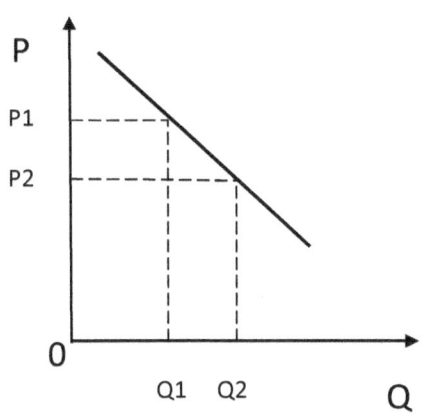

Example:

Price	Quantity Demanded (Qd)
P 15.00	50
P 22.50	25

Ep = (25 – 50) / 50   **Ep = 1**
 (22.50 – 15) / 15

Ep = -25 / 50   **1 = 1 = UNITARY**
 7.50 / 15

Ep = 0.5
  0.5

4. **Perfectly Elastic**

   At a certain price, the percentage change in quantity demanded can change many times if not infinitely. Perfectly Elastic is used only in Demand. *Infinitely Elastic* is the term use in Supply which basically has the same definition as this one in Demand.

   Graphical representation:

   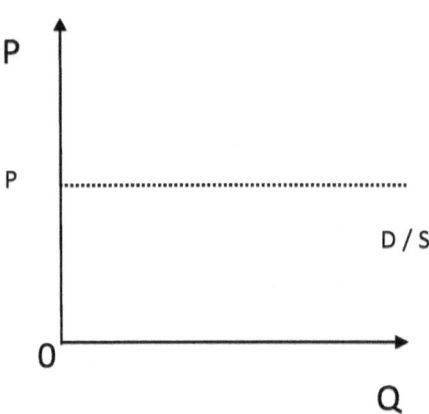

5. **Perfectly Inelastic**

   In here, any change in price does not create any change in quantity demanded. Perfectly Inelastic is the term use in Demand. *Zero Elasticity or Fixed Supply* is the term use in Supply.

   Graphical representation:

   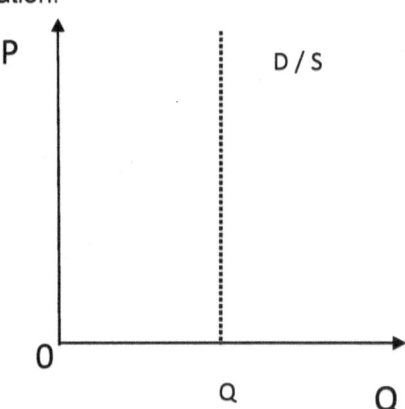

Activity 1: Elasticity

Compute for the Elasticity for the following numbers and indicate what type of elasticity response is produced (Elastic, Inelastic or Unitary). Show your solutions.

1. P_1 = P 20.50 Q_1 = 180
   P_2 = P 23.75 Q_2 = 145

2. P_1 = P 5.00 Q_1 = 120
   P_2 = P 4.75 Q_2 = 140

3. P_1 = P 750.00 Q_1 = 200
   P_2 = P 775.00 Q_2 = 185

4. P_1 = P 185.00 Q_1 = 750
   P_2 = P 200.00 Q_2 = 690

5. P_1 = P 1.25 Q_1 = 105
   P_2 = P 2.50 Q_2 = 100

Activity 2: Graphical representations.

Using the figures in Activity 1, plot the figures in the graphs provided and indicate whether they are Supply or Demand.

1.
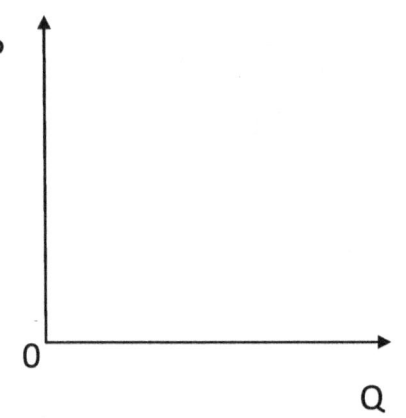

2.
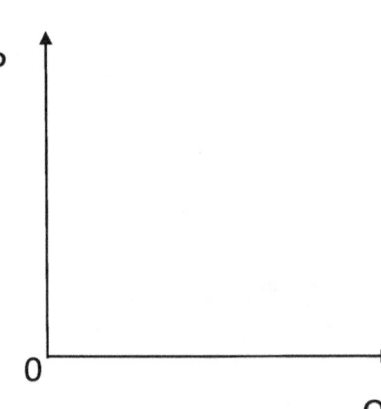

3.
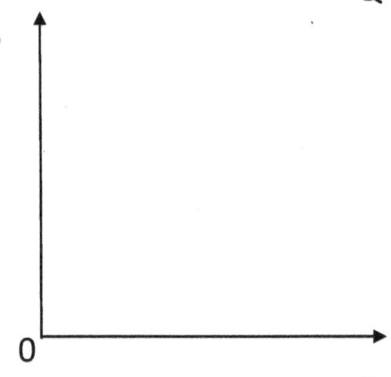

4.
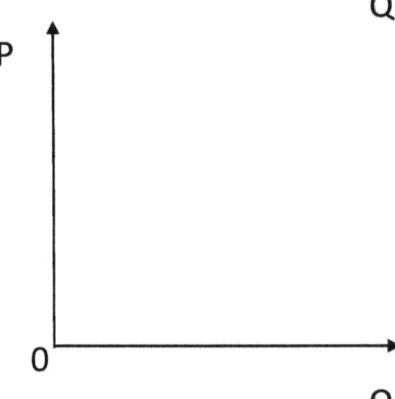

5.
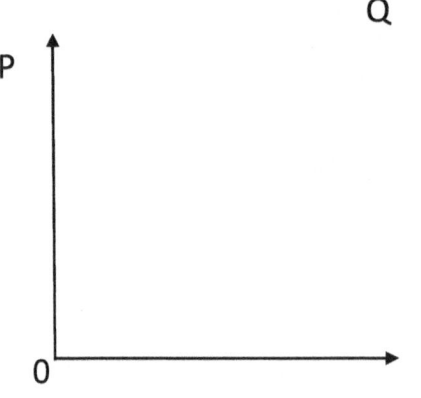

Activity 3: Problem Solving

Determine the elasticity in the given situations and indicate whether if it's elastic, inelastic or unitary. Show your solutions.

Demand Schedule

Situation	Price (P)	Quantity Demanded (Qd)
A	82	310
B	89	302
C	92	295
D	113	257
E	125	220
F	159	155

1. Situations A & E
   P1 =   Qd1 =
   P2 =   Qd2 =

2. Situations B & C
   P1 =   Qd1 =
   P2 =   Qd2 =

3. Situations D & F
   P1 =   Qd1 =
   P2 =   Qd2 =

Supply Schedule

Situation	Price (P)	Quantity Supplied (Qs)
A	87	784
B	94	801
C	117	812
D	123	847
E	142	863
F	161	884

1. Situations B & E
   P1 =   Qs1 =
   P2 =   Qs2 =

2. Situations C & F
   P1 =   Qs1 =
   P2 =   Qs2 =

3. Situations A & D
   P1 =   Qs1 =
   P2 =   Qs2 =

Chapter 4: Market Economy

Industry

This is the term refers to a group of companies that are related in terms of their primary business activities. In modern economies, there are dozens of different industry classifications, which are typically grouped into larger categories called sectors.

Individual companies are generally classified into industries based on their largest sources of revenue. For example, an automobile manufacturer might have a small financing division that contributes 10% to overall revenues, but the company will still be universally classified as an auto maker for attribution purposes. (http://www.investopedia.com/)

Industrial Economics

This is the study of firms, industries, and markets. Industrial Economics aims to aid business men and economists in their decision making in the following areas:

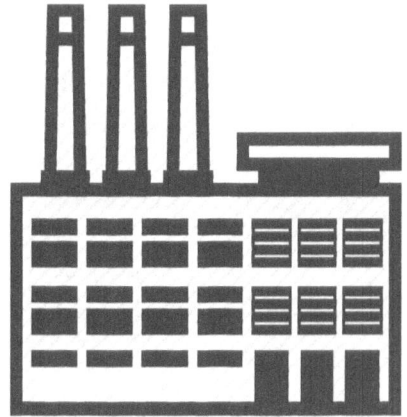

1. How firms should invest in research and development
2. Hoe firms should identify their target market and how they should advertise to attract their desired consumers.
3. How firms organize their activities and considered what their motivation is for doing a particular activity.

An issue in industrial economics is in assessing or evaluating how competitive a market is. Competitive Markets happen when there are a large number of producers or sellers who compete with one another to satisfy the needs and wants of an even larger number of consumers. These competitive markets are normally good for the consumers because the wider range of identical goods which they could freely choose from. In here, competition among producers is natural for they sell identical or generic products. This means one company's product can be a substitute for another company's product.

They compete on quality, value for money, quantity, and most important of all, price. Companies in a competitive market rely heavily in market share and advertising.

In the study of Economics, Self-Interest is identified as the prime motivator of Economic Activity. This is also the primary cause of competition in sellers and also in buyers. *Self-Interest* is identified as the seeking of personal gains of individuals. As said in the previous statements, it is not just applicable to sellers but also to buyers. This is seen in buyers when they are competing to gain the benefit of a good or a service. This is especially true when there are sales or promos. An example of which is the 'Piso Fair' of Cebu Pacific Air. This is observed in the sellers each time they perform the service they are offering. They do not perform for you out of their kindness, not out of their generosity not even because they really like to do you a favor. They perform a service for you because of their vested Self-Interest. They will gain something because of their accomplishment of a service for you.

"It is not from the kindness of the butcher, the brewer, or the baker that we expect our dinner, but from *their regard to their OWN interest."* –Anonymous

Is Self-Interest being greedy? Self-Interest does not necessarily imply greed or immoral behavior. It's simply seeking out one's goals. It's not greed to want to put food on the table for your family. It's not greed for wanting to provide for your loved ones and for one's self. Self-Interest becomes greed if it becomes excessive.

If Self- Interest is the motivator of Economic Activity, *Competition* is the regulator of Economic Activity. It is a check on self-interest by restraining one's ability to take advantage of one's customers. Competition regulates not just economic activity but also the ability to purchase and sell of buyers and sellers respectively. It makes most sellers obliged to provide high quality goods or services at a reasonable price. Competition is the regulator and is the way for sellers to gain their self interests and that is profit. Sellers attain their goals through competition. Sales, profit and market share, these are the goals of sellers. They achieve these goals by offering the best possible combination of price, quality and service to their customers or clients.

Principles in the Formation of Competitive Markets

1. **The Profit Motive**

    Profits are earned when firms gain revenue which exceeds the costs of production. Additional studies in economics identified to two types of profit. First is Normal Profit. Normal profit happens when revenues equal costs. Second is Supernormal Profit. This happens when revenues exceed costs.

2. **The Principle of Diminishability**

    This is the diminishing of stocks of goods as the good is continuously purchased. Prices will be driven upward for it shall follow the Law of Demand where a product's price increases as it nears depletion of its stocks. Higher prices create an incentive for the producers to increase production.

3. **The Principle of Rivalry**

    Consumers are forced to compete with obtain the benefit of the good or service. It's related to the Principle of Diminishability and it's another way to explain how consumers compete when stocks of a good nears depletion.

4. **The Principle of Excludability**

    This is the exclusion of consumers from gaining the benefit of a product. This is necessary to prevent free-riders. Free-Riders are people who enjoy free stuff and will only consume free stuff even if they can do a purchase. These are the people who are unwilling to pay or sometimes are unable to pay. Free-Riders can prevent the formation of fully fledged markets.

5. **The Principle of Rejectability**

    Consumers can reject goods if they do not need nor want them. A shopper in a supermarket may not pay for a product in his/her shopping basket if she does not need nor want it. And supermarket workers cannot expect for a shopper to pay for a product they placed in her basket if the shopper does not need nor want it.

Activity 1: Industrial Economics

Identify examples or scenarios for the different Principles in the Formation of Competitive Markets. Also identify the industry you're referring to.

Example:
Principle of Rivalry
The rivalry of Globe Telecom and Smart Communications in the Tele-Communications Industry

1. Principle Excludability

_____
_____
_____

2. Principle of Rejectability

_____
_____
_____

3. Principle of Profit Motivation

_____
_____
_____

4. Principle of Diminishability

_____
_____
_____

Take Home Activity: Rivalries in the Philippine Economy

Identify companies and their rivals in the Philippine Market. Also identify the industry they are competing in. Make short descriptions of each company and cite their strategies on getting ahead of the competition.

Market Structures

Market structure is best defined as the organizational and other characteristics of a market. We focus on those characteristics which affect the nature of competition and pricing – but it is important not to place too much emphasis simply on the market share of the existing firms in an industry (Riley, 2015. http://beta.tutor2u.net/).

Traditionally, the most important features of market structure are:

1. **The number of firms**
2. **The market share of the largest**
3. **The nature of costs**
4. **The degree to which the industry is vertically integrated**
5. **The extent of product differentiation**
6. **The structure of buyers in the industry**
7. **The turnover of customers**

There are six market structures: Pure Competition, Monopolistic Competition, Oligopoly, Monopoly, Monopsony, and Duopoly.

1. Pure Competition

This is also called *Perfect Competition*. This is where the buyers or the consumers dictate the price. Competition is a key term here because it's because of the profit motive that competition occurred in this type of market structure and how this structure is formed. In here producers or sellers produce a generic product. The products are homogenous, which means another seller's product is a perfect substitute for another's product. An example of this is the rice farmers. They produce the same products which is rice.

2. Monopolistic Competition

This is also called *Imperfect Competition*. This is where there are many sellers but the sellers act independently from one another. The products that they sell are also homogenous. They can be perfect substitutes of one another. An example of this would be the companies in the bath soap industry.

3. Oligopoly

There are many buyers and only a few sellers that do not act independently. The products are perfect substitutes and there is a price range that is influenced mostly by the chief players or sellers in the market. An example of this is the Oil industry. There is a price agreement among the oil sellers here in the Philippines. When some raise their pump prices up, others will follow soon. And it's the same when some drop their oil prices.

4. Monopoly

This happens when there are many buyers and only one seller. There are no eligible substitutes for the product that they sell. The seller here normally dictates the price. Only the government can intervene here through laws and regulation. An example of this is the Electric industry. Meralco is the sole seller of the Electricity here in Metro Manila.

5. **Monopsony**

This happens when there are many sellers but there is only one buyer of that product. This market structure is quite rare. An example of this is the relationship of Meralco to the Power Producers. Meralco is the sole buyer of Electricity here in Metro Manila.

6. **Duopoly**

In this market structure, there are many buyers and only two sellers. This is observed in the Philippines in the potable water industry in Metro Manila. Metropolitan Waterworks and Sewerage System (MWSS), and Maynilad Water Services Inc. are the two major sellers of potable water here in Metro Manila.

Perfect and Imperfect Competition Markets

In Pure/Perfect Competition markets, there is the presence of Product Homogeneity and Perfect Information. *Product Homogeneity* is that the products of all firms are perfect substitutes of one another. *Perfect Information* is when buyers and sellers have all the pertinent information regarding the products and how the market functions. While in Monopolistic/Imperfect Competition Markets have Product Differentiation and Selective Information. *Product Differentiation* is when even though products are substitutes of one another they are heavily differentiated by the sellers. This is when *Selective Information* kicks in. Selective Information is when sellers do not tell all the information needed about the product. Advertising plays a key role in this type of market. In advertising, sellers compete for the attention of the consumers. They sell their product in the "best-foot forward" style. Sometimes all that we know of the product are its good traits and not its bad effects.

Activity 1: Market Structures

Give the characteristics of the different market structures. Complete the details asked in the table. The first row has already been answered as your guide.

Market Structures	Number of Sellers	Number of Buyers	Product Differentiation	Determination of Prices	Example
Pure Competition	Many	Many	Homogenous	Buyers determine the price	Rice industry
Monopolistic Competition					
Monopoly					
Monopsony					
Oligopoly					
Duopoly					

Take Home Activity 1: Research on Market Structures

Research on and briefly discuss the background, current owner/s, rival companies and status of the following companies. Write your answers on the space provided.

1. Jollibee, McDonald's, Wendy's, and Shakey's, (Monopolistic Competition)

   _____
   _____
   _____
   _____
   _____
   _____
   _____
   _____
   _____
   _____
   _____
   _____
   _____

2. Globe Telecomm and Smart Communications (Duopoly)

   _____
   _____
   _____
   _____
   _____
   _____
   _____
   _____
   _____
   _____
   _____
   _____

3. GMA 7, ABS-CBN 2, and TV 5 (Oligopoly)

_____
_____
_____
_____
_____
_____
_____
_____
_____
_____

Take Home Activity 2: Monopoly on the Electric Industry

Briefly define the following Meralco Billing types and then see your Meralco bill and identify the type of your billing account.

1. Residential Service (RS) -

2. General Service (GS) -

3. Non-Industrial Service (NIS) -

4. Industrial Service (IS) -

5. Government Hospitals and Metered Streetlights (GHMS) -

6. Flat Streetlighting Service (FS) -

Take Home Activity 3: Case Analysis

Use the Case Study format given in this book. (pp. 29-31)

Great American Monopolies: *AT & T and Microsoft*

AT&T was a government-supported monopoly - a public utility - that would have to be considered a coercive monopoly. Like Standard Oil, the AT&T monopoly made the industry more efficient and wasn't guilty of fixing prices, but rather the potential to fix prices. The break-up of AT&T by Reagan in the 1980s gave birth to the "baby bells". Since that time, many of the baby bells have begun to merge and increase in size in order to provide better service to a wider area. Very likely, the break-up of AT&T caused a sharp reduction in service quality for many customers and, in some cases, higher prices, but the settling period has elapsed and the baby bells are growing to find a natural balance in the market without calling down Sherman's hammer again.

Microsoft, on the other hand, was never actually broken up even though it lost its case. The case against it was centered on whether Microsoft was abusing what was essentially a non-coercive monopoly. Microsoft has been challenged by many companies, including Google, over its operating systems' continuing hostility to competitors' software.

Just as U.S. Steel couldn't dominate the market indefinitely because of innovative domestic and international competition, the same is true for Microsoft. A non-coercive monopoly only exists as long as brand loyalty and consumer apathy keep people from searching for a better alternative. Even now, the Microsoft monopoly is looking chipped at the edges as rival operating systems are gaining ground and rival software, particularly open source software, is threatening the bundle business model upon which Microsoft was built. Because of this, the antitrust case seems premature and/or redundant.

Chapter 5: The Theory of Production

Production

This refers to any economic activity, which combines the four factors of production to form an output that will satisfy consumers. It simple terms it's the act of combining the factors of production by business firms in order to produce goods and services. It is the conversion of inputs into outputs.

The factors of production are the economic resource—Land, Labor, Capital and Entrepreneur. They are combined in the act of production to create products. Products are created to satisfy man's needs and wants. It is anything that can be offered to the market that might satisfy a need or  a want. In this definition of a product, we get the two qualifications of a product: a. It can be offered to the market, and b. It can satisfy a need or a want.

There are three kinds of products.

1. Goods — These are tangible products.
   - They can be perceived by the five senses
2. Services — These are intangible products but are experienced.
3. Ideas — These are intangible products but they indirectly satisfy a person.

The Production Process

This refers to the way products are processed. This refers to how a firm uses the different resources to come up with a final product. This is best illustrated in the IPO Process. 'I' stands for Inputs, 'P' for Process and 'O' for Output. Input refers to the raw materials used for the production of a particular product. These raw materials are to undergo furnishing or further furnishing. This is the Process part. The process part involves the different phases the raw materials need to undergo for them to become final products. The Output is simply the final product. There are some production processes that incur byproducts or other products aside from the desired final product.

The different inputs in production are the factors of production. In the production process they are called the Elements of Input.

1. **Land** – refers to the natural resources. This also refers to our environmental resources like clean air and potable water.
2. **Labor** – this refers to the physical and mental abilities used in the production of goods and services.
3. **Capital** – these are the goods that are used in the production of other goods and services. These include machines, buildings, factories, roads, and the like.
4. **Entrepreneurship** – these are the ideas that are used in the production process. This involves the efforts of the person or persons in incorporating Land, Labor and Capital resources for the creation or production of new goods and services.

Labor Intensive and Capital Intensive Technology

Labor Intensive - This type of technology utilizes more labor resources than capital resources in the production process. Labor intensive stresses on the use of man-power than machineries and equipments. An example of this would be the agricultural sector where human effort is more valuable than equipment and machine use.

Capital Intensive – This type utilizes more capital resources than labor resources in the production process. This uses more machines, equipments and the like in the production of goods and services. Some industries commonly thought of as capital intensive include oil production and refining, telecommunications and transports such as railways and airlines. There are eleven types of capital defined in this book.

1. **Fixed Capital** — An example of this is land
2. **Circulating Capital** — This is continuously used but for only one usage i.e. gas.
3. **Productive Capital** — These are raw materials that are to be used to produce the final product
4. **Lucrative Capital** — This is capital used not for the purpose of production but for other purposes as the entrepreneur wishes.
5. **Consumption Capital** — This is capital used for the purchase of finished goods for use in the production process.
6. **Free Capital** — These are the machines or equipments that are or can be used many times.
7. **Specialized Capital** — This is capital to be used for a specific and specialized purpose
8. **Agricultural Capital** — An example of this are seeds.
9. **Industrial Capital** — This refers to heavy equipments and buildings.
10. **Commercial Capital** — This refers to mobile vehicles used all throughout the production process
11. **Financial Capital** — This refers to anything used in the production in monetary form.

Entrepreneur

This refers to an individual who, rather than working as an employee, runs a small business and assumes all the risk and reward of a given business venture, idea, or good or service offered for sale. The entrepreneur is commonly seen as a business leader and innovator of new ideas and business processes. Entrepreneurs play a key role in any economy. These are the people who have the skills and initiative necessary to take good new ideas to market and make the right decisions to make the idea profitable. The reward for the risks taken is the potential economic profits the entrepreneur could earn. (http://www.investopedia.com/)

An entrepreneur inputs his ideas, properties, time, and talents to the production process. He utilizes the other factors of production to come up with a satisfying good or service. He is the one who decides on the products to be produced, the materials that are to be used in the production process, the process that they will need to undergo to produce the final product, on the type of technology to be used (Labor or Capital Intensive), and the like.

In the production process, decisions are not based specific number of days, months or years but it is based on the ability to vary the quantity of inputs in production (Marcelino, et al. 2010). There are two types of input—Fixed and Variable. *Fixed Inputs* are resources which their quantity cannot be readily changed while *Variable Inputs* are resources which their quantity can be readily changed in response to changes in output. Now we link this to the short run and long run features of production. In *Short Run*, there is at least one (1) fixed input therefore changes in output must be accomplished by changes in the use of variable inputs. While in *Long Run,* is a period of time so long that all inputs are considered variable (Marcelino, et al. 2010).

Law of Diminishing Marginal Productivity (Law of Diminishing Returns)

This Law states that: "When successive unit of variable input is used with a fixed input beyond a certain point, the additional product produced by each additional unit of variable input decreases." This shows us that it's better to stop at a certain point in increasing the same input, or increase a different input, or produce another or an additional product to maximize profit.

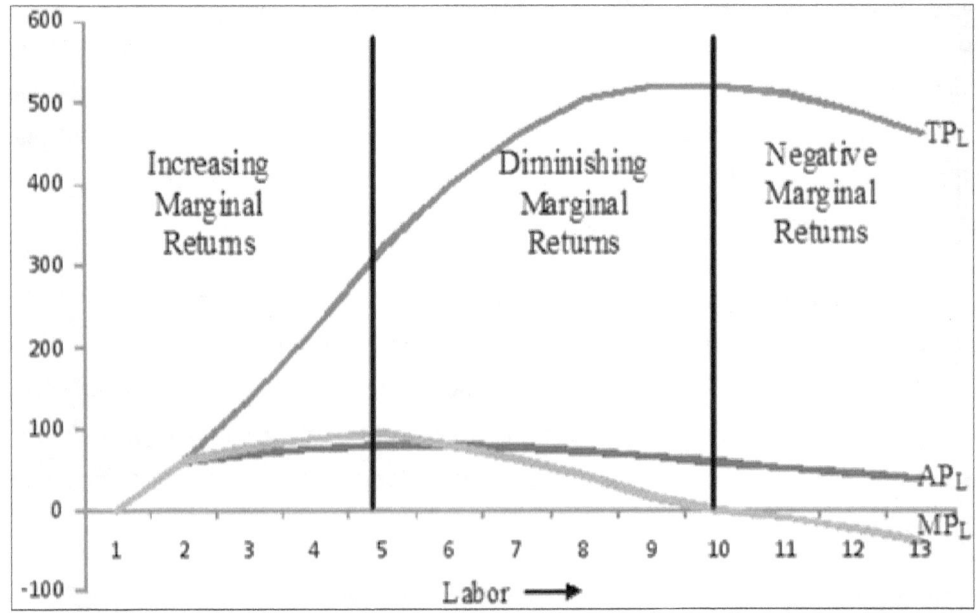

An example from www.investopedia.com, let's consider a pizza restaurant that wants to increase profitability. Increasing the amount of cheese (the input) that goes on each pizza can create a more delicious product and sell more pizzas. But at some point, the pizza reaches an optimal cheese level. The amount of cheese must be balanced with the crust thickness, amount of sauce and other pizza toppings, if any. If the restaurant continues to add more cheese to the pizza beyond the optimal level, its sales will decline because customers will not enjoy pizzas that leave them with a mouthful of cheese and little else. If the pizza restaurant wants to continue to increase its profitability after optimizing the amount of cheese on its pizzas, it might look at increasing a different input, such as pepperoni or sausage, or adding another product, such as chocolate gelato.

Economists compute Marginal Productivity (MP) to see at what point maximum profit is achieved in the production process. Here are the formulas:

Let:

AP = Average Productivity
MP = Marginal Productivity
TP = Total Production
VI = Variable Input

$$AP = \frac{TP}{VI}$$

$$MP = \frac{\Delta TP}{\Delta VI}$$

Here is an example:

VI	TP	AP	MP
1	40	40	40
2	88	44	48
3	138	46	50
4	179	44.75	41
5	200	40	21
6	210	35	10
7	203	29	-7
8	176	22	-27

In the table, the most profitable point in the production is when its Variable Input (VI) is 3. The Average and Marginal Productivity (MP) is at its peak which is 46 and 50 respectively and as the variable input increases from 3, Average and Marginal Product decreases with the Marginal Product decreasing dramatically at Variable Input 8. Productivity is just one factor computed in economics to ensure profitability in the production of goods and services. Another is costs.

The Theory of Cost

Costs of a firm are incurred during the production process. This is due to the purchases of different production resources. There are two classifications of costs in Economics: Fixed and Variable. *Fixed Costs* are expenses that do not change in amount in the whole production process while *Variable Costs* are expenses change in direct proportion to productivity of the business or firm. Variable costs depend on the quantity of output for it is directly proportional to it. Fixed and Variable Costs comprise the *Total Cost* at every point in production.

Here are the formulas used in computing for production costs:

Let:

TP / Output	= quantity of products produced	
TFC	= Total Fixed Cost	
TVC	= Total Variable Cost	
TC	= Total Cost	
AFC	= Average Fixed Cost	
AVC	= Average Variable Cost	
AC	= Average Cost	
MC	= Marginal Cost	

$$TC = TFC + TVC$$

$$AFC = \frac{TFC}{TP}$$

$$AVC = \frac{TVC}{TP}$$

$$AC = AFC + AVC$$

$$MC = \frac{\Delta TP}{\Delta TC}$$

TP	TFC	TVC	TC	AFC	AVC	AC	MC
0	10,000	0	10,000	0	0	0	0
4,000	10,000	10,000	20,000	2.5	2.5	5	0.4
10,000	10,000	20,000	30,000	1	2	3	0.6
15,000	10,000	30,000	40,000	0.67	2	2.67	0.5
19,400	10,000	40,000	50,000	0.52	2.06	2.58	0.44
23,000	10,000	50,000	60,000	0.43	2.17	2.6	0.36

With Total Production at 10,000, there is reached the highest Average Cost and Marginal Cost of 3 and 0.6 respectively. What do these numbers indicate? Marginal Cost indicates the change in total cost when the quantity produced has an increment by unit. In simple term, it is the cost of producing one more good. In the table, as the quantity of product produced increases the Marginal Cost decreases. This means that when the marginal cost increases then decreases, the production has passed its breakeven point. The more products produced the less marginal cost incurred. But there will come a time when it will rise again due to the variability of costs. The point where Marginal and Average Cost is lowest is the point where the production is best maintained.

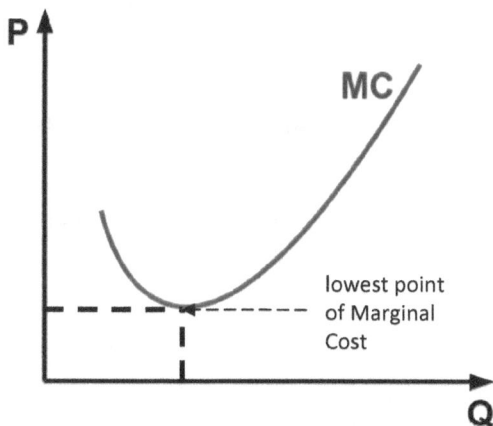

In this graph of Marginal Cost (MC), the point where it is lowest is where costs are maximized and generally, generates more profit for the firm.

Firms usually do this study and computation to find the points in production where additional investments are needed to achieve maximum profit. These investments or additional costs may be in the form of additional capital—raw materials, buildings, machines, equipments, or additional labor—employees, skilled workers, or the increase of both capital and labor resources. This entails additional financial investment which is also added to the cost incurred in production.

Economic Cost

We have discussed cost as part of the production process, now we shall be discussing cost in economics. *Economic Cost* is the sacrifice involved in performing an activity, or following a decision or course of action. This is the cost of employing resources in an economic activity such as production or manufacturing. In here, *Cost* is defined as the burden sustained in order to: (1) perform a particular activity, (2) carry out a certain production, and (3) achieve certain goals. There are five categories of costs:

1. **Actual Costs** — These costs refer to real transactions.
2. **Opportunity Costs** — These are the alternatives taken into consideration. These answer the question 'What must be given up?' to achieve a particular goal or set of goals by decision makers.
3. **Discretionary Costs** — These are the costs for strategic goals, e.g. advertising, improving a company's image, etc.
4. **Attributed Costs** — These are computed values in Accounting. These are the costs that are for the production process of a certain product for purposes of profit (Accounting).
5. **Production Costs** — These are the computed values in Economics. Has the same meaning as Attributed Costs.
    a) **Fixed Costs** — An example of this is the cost of renting an office or a building. There are also Quasi-Fixed Costs. These are the costs incurred for an addiction in a permanent factor in the business. An example of this is the adding of new employees.
    b) **Variable Costs** — These are the costs the vary in the levels of production. They increase or decrease depending in the levels of production.
        a) **Zero Total Cost** = This means there is zero production.

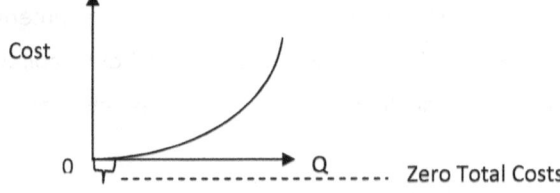

b) **Economies of Scale** = Total cost rises a little less proportional to production. No matter how much is the increase in the variable cost, there will be less and less total cost on the quantity produced.

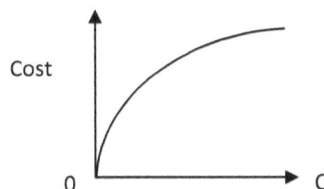

c) **Dis-economies of Scale** = This is the opposite of Economies of Scale. In here, an increase in variable cost equals a great increase in quantity of products produced.

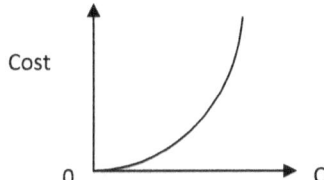

d) **Constant Return to Scale** = In here, there is an exact match of growth in the variable costs to the percentage of total cost.

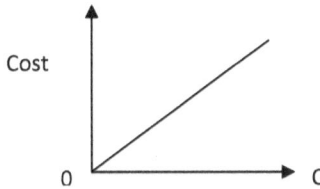

c) **Total Cost** — This is the sum total of all the costs incurred in the production of goods and services
d) **Average Costs** — These are the costs incurred for each part or section of the production process.
e) **Marginal Costs** — These are the costs that indicate how much the Total Cost changes because of the modification in production level by one unit.

Activity 1: Production Theory

On the space provided, write **True** if the statement is correct and **False** if the statement is wrong.

_____ 1. Entrepreneurs combine all the factors in production to create a final goods and services.
_____ 2. Land, water, labor and capital are the four factors in production.
_____ 3. Industrial capital refers to money used in the production process.
_____ 4. Goods, Services and Ideas are all tangible.
_____ 5. Capital refers to all resources, natural and man-made, used in the production of goods and services.
_____ 6. Products are anything that could be offered in the market and satisfy a need or a want.
_____ 7. Ideas are intangible products but do not satisfy an individual.
_____ 8. There are two types of technologies used in the production process.
_____ 9. Labor refers to all the human efforts used in producing goods and services
_____ 10. Capital Intensive technology gives emphasis in the use of more capital resources rather than labor resources.

Activity 2: Marginal Productivity

Solve for AP and MP.

VI	TP	AP	MP
1	110		
5	250		
10	410		
15	570		
20	630		
25	690		
30	720		
35	750		

Activity 3: Marginal Cost

Solve for TC, AFC, AVC, AC, and MC.

TP	TFC	TVC	TC	AFC	AVC	AC	MC
100	8, 700	250					
1000	8, 700	500					
3200	8, 700	1, 000					
7450	8, 700	2, 000					
14440	8, 700	4, 000					
16220	8, 700	6, 000					
17000	8, 700	8, 000					

Take Home Activity 1: Marginal Productivity Case Study

Directions: *Use the Case Study Format on pp. 29-31 in writing your analysis for this case. At the end of the case, explain how XEROX improved efficiency and international competitiveness.*

Japan is tough but Xerox prevails.

When the Xerox Corporation began designing its new high-speed photocopying machine, the Model 5100, it had world markets in mind, especially the Japanese.

But it took a different tack from American auto makers, which, in pursuit of Japanese markets, tried to sell cars with steering wheels on the wrong side. Xerox took great pains to understand the needs of its foreign customers, developing a machine for the Japanese that would duplicate the delicate kanji language characters, for instance, or would handle the flimsy papers used in Japan.

Now the American machine, capable of producing high-quality reproductions faster than anything made by Japanese manufacturers, has become the biggest-selling high-speed paper copier in Japan. A spokesman for Fuji Xerox, an independent affiliate that distributes the 5100 in Japan, said its sales there were approaching 90 percent of the high-speed market. Customers Are Pleased

Xerox's Japanese competitors declined to comment on the success of the American product but the company's Japanese customers are clearly pleased. The NEC Corporation, one of the country's biggest electronics companies, has purchased 22 of the big copiers. "The machines are better than anything we can get in Japan," a spokesman said. "We are not concerned that it is an American product. We wanted the best and most efficient machine."

The Model 5100, the people who built it and the approach they took have played a major part in rescuing an American corporation from damaging competition by the Japanese.

In the early 80's, the situation at Xerox had become so bad that as David T. Kearns, its former chairman, later wrote: "If nothing were done to correct things, we were destined to have a fire sale and close down by sometime in the 1990's." Japanese companies -- Canon, Sharp, Toshiba, Ricoh and Minolta -- had made the company a special target, he said, and were hurting it badly.

Unlike the makers of television sets and other consumer electronic products, many of which closed American factories or sold them to foreign companies, Xerox chose to fight: The strategy was to beat the Japanese at their own game, and Xerox went on a quality binge.

The Xerox approach is by no means trouble free. But by and large management consultants and the company are pleased with the results and believe they hold great promise for American competitiveness.

Chapter 6: Business

In the final chapter of this book, we shall have an introductory discussion about Business. *Business* is where much of economic activity takes place but all of business activities involve economic principles. Business is a system of interrelated activities. These activities may involve production or manufacturing, buying, selling and consuming goods and services for the purposes of profit and satisfaction. But in business, they have three concerns: (1) sales, (2) profit, and (3) market share. *Sales* pertain to the activity of selling and getting money from it. *Profit* comes after sales; it is when the company deducts its cost of manufacturing or procuring the product to the sale of it. And, *Market Share* pertains to the amount of trust they enjoy from their consumers. The first and foremost goal of business is for profit. Self-Interest plays a big part in the concept of business. People establish businesses because they need and want to gain profit.

Basic Forms of Business

1. **Single or Sole Proprietorship**
2. **Partnership**
3. **Corporation**
4. **Cooperative**

Single or Sole Proprietorship

There is only one owner of the business. This is the simplest form of business. This is not a legal entity meaning it does not have a juridical personality. In here, the business is owned by one natural person wherein there is no legal distinction between the owner and the business.

ADVANTAGES	DISADVANTAGES
- all income goes to the owner of the business - centralized management; there is only one boss - easy to organize - easy to increase or decrease capital - less tax burden	- all losses goes to the owner - unlimited liability - limited management expertise - no available capital

Partnership

In the contract of partnership, two or more people bind themselves to contribute money, property or industry to a common fund with the intention of dividing the profits among themselves. The maximum number of partners allowed to enter into a contract of partnership is ten (10). Not all persons are allowed to enter into a contract. First, an *Emancipated Minor* cannot go into a contract. Emancipated mean uncontrolled or unbounded individuals.  By law, minors can go participate in a contract but they should be guided or are bound by their parents or legal guardians in pursuing a contract. Second, *Deaf-Mute* individuals cannot contract. Third, *Insane or Demented persons* are not allowed to participate in a contract. These persons are not in the proper mind set to perform or contribute in a contract which binds them to do, give or perform a task which makes them prone to abuses. This is to protect them from forms of deception or trickery. Lastly, A person suffering from *Civil Interdiction* cannot go into a contract. Persons under civil interdiction are banned or prohibited from participating in some legal procedures and rights. This may be due to a court order or from being penalized by law.

In a partnership, partners contribute for the establishment and operations of the business. Their end goal is for them to gain profit from their endeavor. They mainly contribute three things: (1) Money, (2) Property, and (3) Industry. *Money* refers to the legal tender accepted or prescribed by law or by the state. This includes the negotiable instruments accepted by the state—checks, promissory notes, treasury bills and bonds and the like. *Property* refers to all the material things that readily available to be given as contribution to the partnership. These are all tangible goods, i.e. machines, buildings, office table. *Industry* refers to the intangible goods that a partner may render in service of the partnership. Examples of this are time, ideas, and services.

A partnership being a legal and binding contract acquires a juridical personality which makes it gains the power to sue, be sued, and countersue. Even though the partners are different individuals, there is only one partnership formed and each partner is a partner of the other. These partners do not contribute money, some contribute property and some only contribute industry.

Types of Partners

1. **General Partner** - The partner who holds the biggest interest in the partnership business.
2. **Limited Partner** - This is the partner who has a liability only to his Capital of Contribution.
3. **Industrial Partner** - This is the partner who contributes his services, his ideas to the partnership.
4. **Managing Partner** - The partner who manages the affairs of the partnership venture.

Corporation

This is an artificial being created by operations of law having the right of succession and the powers and attributes expressly authorized by law. A corporation as an artificial being has its own juridical personality. The least amount of members of

incorporators is five (5) and the maximum is fifteen (15). It has a life span of fifty (50) years. It's registration to the Securities and Exchange Commission is renewable five (5) years before its expiration.

In a partnership agreement, partners contribute money, industry and property and are the basis for each partners profit in the business while in a corporation; stocks are the basis in computing for a corporator's profit. *Stocks* are certificates of ownership. Every corporator is a stockholder. *Stockholders* are investors who are part owners of a corporation. There are two classifications of stocks: (1) Common and (2) Preferred. *Common stocks* are the stocks when bought gain for the stockholder voting rights in the corporation while *Preferred stocks* do not make a stockholder gain voting rights when bought. Corporations are classified into two—Stock and Non-stock. *Stock Corporations* are corporations established for profit purposes. Examples of this are SM Prime Holdings Corp., GMA Network Inc., PLDT Communication and Energy Ventures., etc. *Non-stock Corporations* are established for non-profit purposes. Examples are schools, foundations, and the like.

Cooperative

This is a jointly owned enterprise engaging in the production of goods or the supply of services, operated by its members for their mutual benefit, typically organized by consumers or farmers.

Cooperative Principles (http://ica.coop/)

The co-operative principles are guidelines by which co-operatives put their values into practice.

1. Voluntary and Open Membership

Co-operatives are voluntary organizations, open to all persons able to use their services and willing to accept the responsibilities of membership, without gender, social, racial, political or religious discrimination.

2. Democratic Member Control

Co-operatives are democratic organizations controlled by their members, who actively participate in setting their policies and making decisions. Men and women serving as elected representatives are accountable to the membership. In primary co-operatives members have equal voting rights (one member, one vote) and co-operatives at other levels are also organized in a democratic manner.

3. Member Economic Participation

Members contribute equitably to, and democratically control, the capital of their co-operative. At least part of that capital is usually the common property of the co-operative. Members usually receive limited compensation, if any, on capital subscribed as a condition of membership. Members allocate surpluses for any or all of the following purposes: developing their co-operative, possibly by setting up reserves, part of which at least would be indivisible; benefiting members in proportion to their transactions with the co-operative; and supporting other activities approved by the membership.

4. Autonomy and Independence

Co-operatives are autonomous, self-help organizations controlled by their members. If they enter into agreements with other organizations, including governments, or raise capital from external sources, they do so on terms that ensure democratic control by their members and maintain their co-operative autonomy.

5. Education, Training and Information

Co-operatives provide education and training for their members, elected representatives, managers, and employees so they can contribute effectively to the development of their co-operatives. They inform the general public - particularly young people and opinion leaders - about the nature and benefits of co-operation.

6. Co-operation among Co-operatives

Co-operatives serve their members most effectively and strengthen the co-operative movement by working together through local, national, regional and international structures.

7. Concern for Community

Co-operatives work for the sustainable development of their communities through policies approved by their members.

Activity 1: Business Comparison

In a piece of paper, write the advantages and disadvantages of the following business form comparisons.

1. Single Proprietorship and Partnership
2. Partnership and Corporation
3. Single Proprietorship and Corporation

Activity 2: Business

Identify the term being defined. Write your answers on the space provided.

_____ 1. A Non-profit Corporation is also called _____.
_____ 2. This is a jointly owned enterprise engaging in production of goods and/or supply of services for the mutual benefit of its members.
_____ 3. This is the partner who has the biggest interest or share in the partnership contract.
_____ 4. ⎫
_____ 5. ⎬ The three contributions in a partnership.
_____ 6. ⎭
_____ 7. This is the simplest and most numerous form of business used.
_____ 8. This term refers to the investors in a corporation.
_____ 9. This is an artificial being created by operations of law having the right of succession, and powers and attributes as prescribed by law beginning with it having a juridical personality.
_____ 10. This is the partner who contributes his services to the partnership.
_____ 11. Who is liable in the single proprietorship form of business?
_____ 12. Where do Partnerships and Corporations register?
_____ 13. This refers to the legal tender as contribution in a partnership.
_____ 14. What is the life span of a corporation?
_____ 15. These are certificates of ownership in a corporation.

Take Home Activity 1: Case Study: Business Choices

Directions: *Use the Case Study Format on pp. 29-31 in writing your case analysis.*

UPTOWN TREEHOUSE

Founded by Aseem Badshah, **Uptown Treehouse** creates campaigns employing elements for Facebook, Twitter, LinkedIn, StumbleUpon and Outbrain. It helps companies introduce new products and initiatives and has worked, for example, with both Guess Jeans and the television show "Breaking Bad."

While building the company, Mr. Badshah and a programmer, Kevin Yu, created software that searches social media and other Web sources to generate sales leads, and that software has taken on a life of its own. In fact, the lead-generation software was so effective that Mr. Badshah and Mr. Yu created a separate start-up, **Socedo**, to develop and sell the software. Thus far, however, they remain uncertain as to how to finance the start-up and how to divide their time between the two companies, which are in different cities. They believe Socedo, based in Seattle, could earn much larger profits, but with much greater risk.

BACKGROUND:

Mr. Badshah, 24, graduated from the University of Washington in 2010 with a business degree. He moved to Los Angeles with the idea of starting the marketing agency that became Uptown Treehouse.

As part of the promotional campaign for the agency, Mr. Badshah started looking for ways to find sales leads that might turn into clients. His team created software that scanned social media for words that would identify potential customers. Then they used those words to start a conversation with the target customers through social media channels.

When the Microsoft development team was looking for people to create Windows 8 or Windows phone apps, for example, Mr. Badshah's software scanned social Web sites and public forums for people who were commenting on mobile application development and let the development team contact them, offering links to Microsoft resources and connecting them to others who could help them develop new applications. Mr. Badshah found this new referral system more effective than cold-calling for customers.

Inspired, he teamed up with Mr. Yu, a former Microsoft engineer he had met during a University of Washington entrepreneurship event, to start Socedo, choosing the name because it was a combination of social and succeed, and because they considered it short and "brandable."

Over the last year, the programming team has continued to develop the lead-generating software, which is now being tested by some 200 companies — mostly small outfits but also a couple of big names in Mr. Badshah's Seattle hometown, Zillow and Microsoft.

Thus far, Mr. Badshah said, the testing has indicated that some 20 percent of the sales leads Socedo generates for its clients are of high enough quality for those clients to include them in their sales pipelines. With about 10 percent of the companies indicating they are ready to pay for Socedo on a monthly basis, he now hopes to introduce the software for sale in the next few weeks.

www.ingramcontent.com/pod-product-compliance
Lightning Source LLC
Chambersburg PA
CBHW020931180526
45163CB00007B/2973